I want to be

A MAGICIAN

Ivan Bulloch & Diane James

STARRING

MICHAEL

NICOLE

MILTON

KIM

TWO-CAN
in association with
THOMSON LEARNING

Consultant Otis Earle
Photographs © Fiona Pragoff
Illustrations Debi Ani
Design Assistant Peter Clayman

Copyright © Two-Can Publishing Ltd, 1995

First published in the United States
in 1995 by Thomson Learning,
New York NY

Printed and bound by G. Canale and C.S.p.A, Italy

Library of Congress Cataloging-in Publication Data

Bulloch, Ivan.
    A magician / Ivan Bulloch & Diane James.
        p.   cm. —— (I want to be)
    Includes index.
    Summary: A how-to book on magic with detailed illustrations for a
variety of tricks.
    ISBN 1-56847-365-6 (HC)
    1. Conjuring——Juvenile literature. 2. Tricks——Juvenile literature.
3. Magicians——Juvenile literature. [1. Magic tricks.] I. James, Diane. II. Title.
III. Series: Bulloch, Ivan. I want to be.
GV1548.B85   1995
793.8——dc20   95-10669

CONTENTS

I WANT TO BE . . . 4

IT'S SO EASY! . . . 6

PAPER MAGIC . . . 8

HATS OFF! . . . 10

SECRET STRETCH . . . 12

MAGIC TUBES . . . 14

VANISHING COIN . . . 16

IT'S A SNIP! . . . 18

BODY POWER . . . 20

WANNA BET? . . . 22

SNAP! . . . 24

SECRET SHELF . . . 26

BEFORE THE SHOW . . . 28

SHOW TIME . . . 30

I WANT TO BE A MAGICIAN

As soon as your friends discover your amazing new skills, they will want you to perform for them. You'll need to set aside quite a bit of time for practicing to perfect your act. Always remember the golden rule: NEVER tell anyone how a trick is performed. Also, remember that performing the same trick twice in a row is asking for trouble!

Make a special hat to help the magic work!

Even simple props, like a piece of string and a pair of scissors, can be used to make magic!

4

Making something appear as if from nowhere is one of the best tricks you can do!

All magicians have a few card tricks up their sleeve.

Some tricks need to be set up beforehand – like this secret shelf!

When you have learned enough tricks, you can put on a show for your friends. Later in the book you will find some tips to help with the preparations.

IT'S SO EASY!

Some tricks are so simple you can perform them anywhere! Good magicians always have plenty of pockets to keep props handy.

Pencil power

This is a really snappy trick, and all you need is a rubber band and a pencil. Choose a rubber band that is as close to your skin color as possible.

Attach the pencil to the back of your hand with the rubber band. Don't let the audience see the pencil. Tell them you can make a pencil appear out of thin air.

Flick your wrist down quickly and the pencil will appear as if by magic.

The invisible ball

Hold the edge of a paper bag as though you were going to snap your fingers. Ask someone to throw an imaginary ball into the bag. Just as the ball is about to land in the bag, snap your fingers and pretend to catch the ball. The noise will sound just like a real ball falling into the bag!

Don't let anyone see this side of your hand.

PLOP!

Double your money

This trick will take a few seconds to set up. Open a magazine and lay three coins on a page. Turn over a couple of pages to cover up the coins. Tell a friend that you can magically double his money.

Ask him to put three coins on the empty page. Close the magazine. Say the magic words and gently shake the magazine. Out will fall six coins.

Stubborn pencil

This is an amazingly easy trick, but very effective. Stand sideways to your audience and put a pencil on the palm of one hand. Using the other hand, grip your wrist.

Turn the hand with the pencil so that the audience sees only the back of it. As you turn your hand, secretly place your forefinger on the pencil. This will keep it in position. The audience will think the pencil is refusing to let go of you!

PAPER MAGIC

It's just amazing what you can do with a few pieces of paper! You can make a tree appear in a flash and create two separate rings from one strip of paper.

Paper palm tree
Roll a sheet of newspaper up starting from one of the short ends.

Secure the end with a piece of tape.

Using a pair of scissors, make cuts through all the layers. Start at one end of the roll and cut to about halfway down. After a bit of practice, you will be able to do all of this easily in a matter of seconds.

Now for the real magic! With a big flourish, gently pull up the center layers. As you pull, you will gradually reveal a giant palm tree!

Use colored wrapping paper instead of newspaper for an extra-special tree

8

Paper rings

Tell your audience that you can turn a single strip of paper into two interlinked loops. All you need is a pair of scissors and some clear tape.

Take the strip of paper and make two twists in it. Tape the ends together.

I surprise myself every time I do this trick!

Using the scissors, cut the loop you have made lengthwise down the middle. Keep going all the way around. Now for the magic!

When you pull the loop apart you will have two rings joined together!

HATS OFF!

Every magician needs a hat! A hat will help you feel the part and show your audience that you are a professional.

Here are some ideas for making your own hats. You'll need thin colored cardboard for the top hat, and sticky back felt and thin cord for the fez. You'll also some scissors and glue.

Top hat

Decide how tall you want your hat. Cut a rectangle of card to this height, and make sure it is long enough to go around your head. Glue the ends together to make a cylinder. Draw around one end of the hat and cut out a circle of cardboard to make the top.

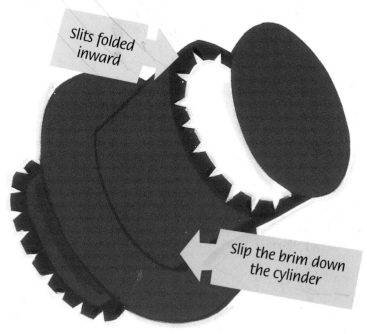

Slits folded inward

Slip the brim down the cylinder

For the brim, draw around one of the ends again. Then draw a wider circle around it. Cut around both circles. Now make slits at both ends of the cylinder. Fold in the slits at the top and fold out the slits at the bottom. Put glue on the top surfaces of the slits. Stick the top of the hat on, then slip the brim down the cylinder.

Cut glittery stars from wrapping paper or foil and glue them on.

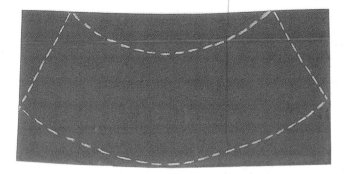

To finish off your fez, make a tassel. Wind some thin black cord around and around a rectangle of cardboard. Slip the cord off the card carefully. Tie a short piece of cord around one end to make a loop. Cut through the cord at the other end.

Fez

Take a piece of sticky back felt about 24 inches long and cut a shape like the one above. Cut a piece of cardboard the same size. Stick the two together. Curve the shape around your head. Glue the edges together. Make slits around the top edge and fold them in.

Don't use too much card or it will be difficult to cut.

Use a needle and thread to attach the tassel to the top of your fez.

Glue the circle to the tabs.

Draw around the top of your hat and cut out a circle from felt and cardboard.

SECRET STRETCH

The secret ingredient in both of these tricks is a piece of elastic. It can make a key seem to vanish and a magic wand appear to rise of its own free will!

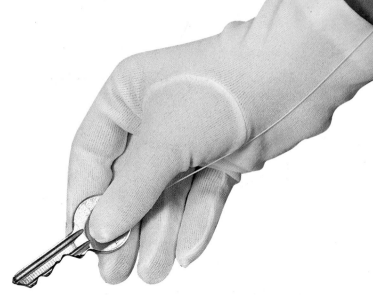

Pull the key out with your right thumb and first finger and hold it on the palm of your left hand. Don't let your audience see the elastic.

Make sure the safety pin is secure.

Keep that elastic well hidden!

Vanishing key
Tie one end of a piece of elastic – about 12 inches long – to a key, and the other end to a large safety pin. Attach the safety pin to the top of your right jacket sleeve. You may need to adjust the pin to make sure that the key does not show below your sleeve.

Pretend that you are taking the key in your left hand by making a fist. Let the key whizz back out of sight up your sleeve. Now show the audience both hands. Where is the key?

Magic wand

No matter how many times you push this wand back down in your hand, it still insists on rising back up again!

Make a show of "talking" to the wand. Tell it to stop playing around!

Cut a 10-inch length of plastic tubing. You can buy this from a hardware store. You also need two white buttons with shanks, exactly the same diameter as the tubing, and an 8-inch piece of elastic. Glue black paper around the wand and add short strips of white paper at either end.

Take one of the buttons between your thumb and first finger and pull the button and elastic down and up along the side of the wand. Grip the wand tightly and make sure the audience cannot see the elastic.

Attach one of the buttons to the elastic and thread the elastic through the tubing. Pull the elastic out through the other end and attach the other button. The elastic should now be taut.

Make your magic wand rise on its own by slowly releasing your grip on it. The elastic will push the wand up as it goes back into the tubing.

MAGIC TUBES

This trick will take some time to prepare, but it's well worth the effort. You are bound to get plenty of applause!

Magic tubes

You can make a bottle of mouth-watering orange soda appear from nowhere! You'll need one sheet each of blue and red paper and three sheets of black paper. Each should measure 24 inches wide and 10 inches long.

| ← 6½ in. → | ← 11 in. → | ← 6½ in. → |

Glue the sheet of blue paper to a sheet of black paper. Using the illustration above as a guide, cut a pattern of holes through both pieces. Bring the short ends together to make a tube and glue them.

Make a similar tube — but 9½ inches long — from the red and black paper. Overlap the short ends to make a slightly narrower tube. Do the same thing with the remaining sheet of black paper, again making the tube slightly shorter and narrower.

Set up the tubes before your audience arrives. Put the black tube on the table with the bottle of orange soda inside it. Cover it with the red tube and then the blue tube.

Make sure the holes face your audience

When you have your audience's attention, lift off the blue tube and hold it up so that they can see that it is black inside. Put your hand through it to show it is empty. Replace it over the red tube.

The audience will not be able to see the black tube. They will think it is the inside of the blue tube.

Look carefully! There is nothing whatsoever inside this tube.

Now lift out the red tube and show that it, too, is empty. Wave your magic wand, say the magic words, and pull the bottle out of the black tube!

You can make all sorts of things appear magically, but make sure that they will fit in the black tube.

VANISHING COIN

Simple to prepare and even easier to perform, this trick will baffle your audience! There is plenty of scope for some good magicians patter.

Circle of felt or paper to make a false top

Use a glass that is not too tall and will fit comfortably in your hand.

Make sure you can slip the cover on and off easily.

Getting ready

Cover a square of cardboard with some colored felt or paper. Or, simply lay the felt or paper on a table top. Using the same color, draw around the rim of a glass and cut out a circle. Glue the circle to the rim of the glass so that it has a false top. Make a paper cover to fit around the glass from paper of a different color.

The trick

Tell your audience that you are going to make a coin disappear. Show them the board, the glass without the cover, the cover, and the coin.

Be careful that your audience doesn't see the false top of the glass.

With a little flourish, put the cover over the glass. Then place the glass with its cover over the coin. Wave your wand over the glass and say some magic words.

Lift the cover carefully off the glass and — surprise, surprise — the coin has vanished completely! Your audience won't believe how easily you have performed this trick. Of course, you know that the coin is really hidden by the false top on the glass.

Be careful not to nudge the glass when you put the cover on.

You saw it with your very eyes! Where has it gone?

Now you can baffle your audience again by making the coin reappear. Simply do the trick in reverse. Put the cover back on the glass.

Grip the cover and glass firmly so the glass doesn't slip out.

Say the magic words and lift both the glass and its cover in one movement. The coin that was hidden appears magically! As with all magic tricks, don't let the audience persuade you to do it again.

IT'S A SNIP!

A pair of scissors is the most important prop for these two impressive tricks. You will also need a steady hand and lots of practice!

Cut and mend

Hold a length of cord between your thumb and first finger. Take a short piece of the same cord and make it into a loop. Hide it as shown. With your other hand take the bottom of the long loop and tuck it up under your thumb. At the same time, push the short loop up.

The audience can now see the top of the short loop.

Use a pair of scissors to cut through the short loop. The audience will think you have cut through your long loop! Trim off all the ends, letting the short loop fall to the floor with the other pieces.

This is the side of your hand that the audience never sees.

The audience knows nothing about the secret short loop!

Ask someone in the audience to pull the end of the cord nearest them. Presto! It is still in one piece!

Magic envelope

First prepare your envelope. Cut a small hole out of the back and two slits at either side.

THIS is the side the audience sees.

Never let the audience see this side!

Make it look as though you are struggling to cut through the cord.

Thread a piece of cord through the slits. You will be able to see it through the small hole. Now the trick is prepared and ready to try out on your audience.

Tell your audience that you are going to cut through the envelope and cord. Before you start, secretly pull out a loop of cord through the hole at the back. Put the blade of the scissors *under* this loop and cut through the envelope. Invite someone to pull an end of the cord. They will be amazed to find it in one piece!

You can use ribbon, but make sure the slits and hole are big enough.

Keep the blade of the scissors under the cord.

BODY POWER

Your body has its own magic. You just need to know how to unlock it. Here are a few tricks to astound your friends.

Tell a friend or someone in your audience that you can make sausages appear in front of their very eyes! Ask them to hold their index fingers, touching, in front of their eyes and stare hard at the spot where they join. The sausages will appear after a few seconds.

> With just the power in my magic finger I can keep you from getting off that chair!

> Help! I'm seeing flying sausages!

Move your fingers apart to make a floating sausage!

Magic finger

Ask someone to sit all the way back on a straight-backed chair and hold the edges of the seat. Stand in front and press your first finger against their forehead. Challenge them to get up. They will be amazed to find that all their strength seems to have gone!

20

1,2,3 . . . oops!

You have the magic power to make people fall over without even touching them! Tell two people to stand with one leg slightly raised and count to ten. They will be able to do this easily. Now tell them you can make them fall over. Put blindfolds around their eyes and move away. Ask them to raise their leg again and count to ten. By the time they get to 3 or 4 they will be wobbling all over the place!

Moving pencil

Hold a pencil at arm's length and line it up with something in the distance. Shut each eye in turn. The pencil will jump from side to side!

Some unknown force is making my pencil move!

WANNA BET?

All magicians have a few card tricks up their sleeves. This one and the one on the next page depend on remembering a "key" card.

Fanning cards out like this is useful for lots of tricks.

Pick someone out of the audience to be a helper. Give your helper a big welcome and ask her to shuffle a pack of cards well.

Fan the pack out face down and ask your helper to pick a card and remember it.

Key card on bottom, helper's chosen card on top

Make sure nobody sees you looking at the key card.

As the helper hands the pack back, sneak a quick glance at the bottom card. Make sure no one sees you looking! The card you have glimpsed is called the key card, and it is very important that you remember it until the end of the trick.

Gather the cards into a neat pile, making sure that the key card is on the bottom. Tell your helper to put her chosen card back face down on top of the pack.

Cut the pack by taking the top half and placing it face down on the table. Put the remaining cards, also face down, on top.

Now is the time to offer your bet. Tell your helper that you bet that the next card you pick will be her card. Of course your helper will think you've got it wrong and will accept the bet eagerly. For the finale, ignore the card in your hand and with a flourish turn over the correct card on the table!

This is one bet I know for sure I'll win!

The key card will now be on top of the chosen card. The helper's chosen card will move to the middle of the pack.

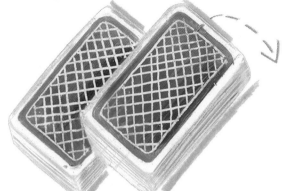

Tell your helper that you are now going to find her chosen card. Start dealing the cards face up in a line. When you turn over the key card, you'll know that the next one will be the chosen card. Don't say anything yet! Turn over a few more cards, getting more and more excited.

SNAP!

Here is another amazing card trick that depends on a key card. You will need two packs of cards – one for yourself and one for your chosen helper.

Tell your helper that you can read his mind and that because of this you will end up choosing *exactly* the same cards. Explain that he should do exactly what you do.

Shuffle a pack of cards and make sure that your helper does the same. Take a quick, secret look at the bottom card of your pack. This is the all-important key card.

Swap packs with your helper. Fan your cards out face down and choose a card. Tell your helper to do the same with his pack and to remember what the card is, keeping it a secret.

I must remember the key card.

Stare deeply into your helper's eyes.

The only card *you* have to remember is the key card. Both of you should gather your packs together and put your chosen cards on top of each pack. Now you should both cut your packs and swap again.

24

Tell your helper to look at his pack and find his chosen card. At the same time, look through your pack to find the key card. The card to the right of the key card is the one your helper chose.

This is the key card.

This is the chosen card.

You chose the Queen of Hearts!

Lay it face down on the table and tell your helper to lay his chosen card next to it. When you turn over the two cards they will be exactly the same and there will be amazement all around!

TIPS

★ When you are taking a quick glimpse at the key card, try diverting your audience's attention by talking to them.
★ Practice shuffling, cutting, and spreading cards into a fan.

SECRET SHELF

With just a little preparation, you can set up a simple trick that will completely baffle your audience. You could use it for the grand finale!

Gather a few small objects. Put them in the middle of a square scarf and gather up the edges. Slip a rubber band around the four corners to secure the bundle. Put the bundle on the secret shelf.

Place bundle on secret shelf.

Put candy and small toys inside the bundle.

The shelf

To make the secret shelf, you'll need a small, sturdy cardboard box, such as a shoe box. Cut a section from the box like the one in the picture above.

Look for a large cardboard box to make into a magic table for the show. Tape or glue the secret shelf to the back of your magic table. Cover it all with a large tablecloth or piece of fabric. Make sure the shelf is covered by the magic cloth so your audience cannot see it.

Now for the easy part. Dip your hand into the hat and slip the rubber band off the bundle. Produce the scarf and all the other objects one after the other. The audience will be amazed. The hat was empty just a few seconds ago!

No, I'm sorry I can't tell you how to do this trick – it's magic!

Let the audience see that your hat is completely empty and then place it, brim down, on the table. Grip the hat by the brim. As you lift it, grab the top of the bundle between your thumb and the brim. Swing the bundle into the hat as it is turned over. This part needs lots of practice so that you can do it in one smooth movement.

BEFORE THE SHOW

Now you are an expert magician. You know how to do lots of different tricks, and it's time to try them out in front of a real audience.

Let everyone know
Decide on a date for your show, making sure you have plenty of time to organize everything. Send invitations to your friends telling them where and when the show will take place. Posters are also a good way of spreading the word.

Planning the program
Don't make your show last too long. Your audience will get tired and you may start making mistakes. Have a pause for refreshments halfway through. Write a list of the tricks you will be performing. Start with something impressive but not too difficult to get into the swing of things.

Make your own posters and invitations using paints and colored paper.

1. secret stretch
2. Vanishing coin
3. Body Magic

Word perfect
Practice your tricks over and over. Try performing in front of a mirror and use your best friends and family for a trial run. You could put on a full-scale dress rehearsal the day before your show.

I'll be glad when it's time for the show!

Be organized
You will probably need quite a few props for your show. Make sure you have exactly what you need beforehand and lay things out so you know where they are.

A special stage will make your performance look extra-professional. Make your own from large sheets of cardboard covered with colored paper.

What do I have to do?

A prop box is good for keeping things together.

He looks like a star!

Don't forget the magic hat!

SHOW TIME

It's time for the show! Make sure you wake up early so you can have a final run-through of your tricks. Check to make sure all your props are in the right place.

THE MORE YOU PRACTICE, THE BETTER YOUR PERFORMANCE WILL BE!

★

WRITE OUT A LIST OF PROPS SO THAT YOU DON'T FORGET ANYTHING.

★

NEVER, EVER GIVE AWAY A MAGIC TRICK.

★

DON'T WORRY IF SOMEONE IN THE AUDIENCE THINKS THEY KNOW HOW YOU HAVE DONE A TRICK. MAKE A JOKE OF IT AND KEEP GOING.

Ladies and gentlemen, I'd like to introduce you to Marvelous Milton. He'll amaze you with his extraordinary magic powers!

A good introduction will set the scene and get the audience excited.

Good magicians need good assistants! Apart from setting up the props beforehand, they can assist throughout the performance by passing props and helping when another pair of hands is needed.

Helpers should also dress up for the performance.

I can see inside your mind! I even know what card you are going to choose. Let me prove it!

If you appear to be confident and in control of things, your audience will be convinced that you really do have magic powers. Starting with a trick that you are particularly good at will help give you the confidence to go on to some of your more difficult ones.

Magic wand to give you special power

Props arranged so you know exactly where everything is

Jacket with pockets inside and outside!

Keep up your patter with the audience. It will help to involve them. Pause when people applaud your amazing skill and never let anyone persuade you to repeat a trick.

Make your table look special by covering it with a long piece of fabric.

"Magic" stage made from cardboard and paper stars

INDEX

assistant 30
card tricks 22, 23, 24, 25
cord trick 18
double your money 7
dress rehearsal 28
fez 10, 11
floating sausages 30
glass 16, 17
invitation 28
key 12
key card 22, 23, 24, 25
magic envelope 19
magic tube 14, 15
magic wand 13, 16, 31
magician's rule 4

paper palm tree 8
paper rings 9
pencil power 6
pockets 6, 31
poster 28
program 28
props 29, 30
scissors 8, 9, 18, 19
secret shelf 26
show 28, 29, 30, 31
stage 29
stubborn pencil 7
top hat 10, 27, 29
vanishing coin 16
vanishing key 12

ABRACADABRA!
I'm about to disappear.
GOODBYE!